TO

SOFIA

LOVE FROM

MUM

Sofia dreamed of becoming an astronaut.

She loved rockets.
She knew more about the Moon than her teachers.
And she had collected loads of space toys.

But today Sofia had to think about making space rather than outer space. Her bedroom was so messy it looked like an asteroid had hit it.

Sofia carefully sorted through everything and began to fill her rucksack with old toys to take to the shed.

12 1 2 3 4 5 6 7 8 9 10 11

Sofia shuffled out of the house and down the garden path.

And there, resting on a pile of broken planks that used to be the shed, was a shiny metal rocket.

"Woah!" yelled Sofia.

"A SPACE ROCKET! IN MY GARDEN!"

Sofia charged up the ramp and clambered up a ladder to the control room. There was a chair in the centre, and she sat down and spun round and round.

As the chair turned she couldn't believe what she was seeing....

Flashing lights, blinking buttons and long levers surrounded her, and a small alien was hunched over, pulling at the controls.

"Err … hello?" said Sofia.

The alien turned round and yelped in surprise. He jumped backwards and sat down on the shiniest, reddest button Sofia had ever seen.

The doors slid shut with a *WHOOSH* and a *CLUNK*, and Sofia felt a rumbling that got bigger and bigger and louder and louder.

5 … 4 … 3 … 2 … 1 …

"Hold on tight!" the alien yelled. "We're off …"

LAUNCH
WHEERRPP!!

"... TO THE MOON!"

As they flew through space they quickly became best friends.

The alien told Sofia amazing stories about his travels through the galaxy, and how today he was heading to the dark side of the Moon. He was sure no one had ever explored it before.

The rocket touched down, and after finding a space suit for Sofia to wear they opened the door.

At the last moment Sofia ducked back inside, quickly tipped her rucksack out and pulled it on. Just in case.

"You never know, it may come in handy," she said.

Sofia and the alien bounced around, kicking up puffs of Moon dust and gazing out at the twinkling stars.

"Hang on," said Sofia, as she took a giant leap, "I think I can see ... tyre tracks?!"

"Maybe we're not the first to explore the dark side of the Moon after all," whispered the alien.

"Only one way to find out," replied Sofia.

They followed the tyre tracks around small craters and huge boulders until they came to the edge of a deep cave.

"What's that at the bottom?" wondered Sofia. The alien slowly lowered her down on the end of a rope, her footsteps echoing around the walls.

CLUMP CLUMP CLUMP **CLUMP** CLUMP CLUMP

"It looks like a metal glove." She stuffed it in her rucksack and quickly climbed back out.

"This will look great in my space-junk collection!" Sofia cheered.

Soon they came to a spooky Moon cave. The alien looked nervous as he peered into the gloom.

"Don't worry," said Sofia as she rummaged in her rucksack, "I've got my old wind-up rocket torch."

They crept into the vast cave and saw crystals covering every wall from top to bottom. As Sofia was gazing up at the sparkling rocks, she stubbed her toe on something and yelped loudly:

"OUCHYA!"

She knelt down to get a closer look: "Hmm, it's a small wheel."

Sofia stuffed it into her rucksack and they trudged up a narrow slope that led back to the surface.

They soon found themselves on the edge of a canyon. Sofia stared hard – she could see a mini satellite dish glinting on the other side.

"Well, we can't go around it," said the alien. "And I don't think we can jump that far, even with a run-up."

"I've got it!" yelled Sofia, as she gripped the valve on her air tank. "Grab my hand and hold tight."

Sofia let out a sudden blast of air and they flew across the canyon, floating gently down on the other side.

"Awesome," she smiled. "I'm going to have the best space-treasure collection ever!"

Sofia was zipping up her rucksack when the alien tapped her on the shoulder.

She looked up and saw the tyre track leading to a huge boulder that had a ginormous shadow stretching out from behind it. The alien gasped:

"YIKES! RUN!"

"Don't worry," said Sofia. "Just stay very, very still...."

As they froze, a cute robot slowly wobbled out from behind the rock, blinking in surprise.

"Hello," smiled Sofia, "are you okay?"

"Hurrr-errr, not really," yawned the space robot. "I've been sleepwalking again and lost a few bits and pieces on the way."

He held out an arm which was missing a hand. He pointed to his leg which was missing a wheel, and then pointed to the side of his head which was missing a mini satellite dish. Sofia gasped.

"HANG ON!"

They carefully took the missing parts out of Sofia's rucksack one by one, while the space robot happily whirred and beeped.

Sofia and the alien helped repair their new friend, and soon the space robot looked his shiny best again.

Out of the corner of her eye Sofia could see Earth, and realised just how much she missed being there: "I think it's time to go home."

They said goodbye to the space robot and began their journey back to the rocket, following their own footsteps.

Over the canyon they went, back through the spooky Moon cave, and around the edge of the deep cave. Soon they were safely back in the control room of the rocket, ready to ...

They slowly rumbled out of the sky into Sofia's garden. The door opened and she walked down the ramp and turned to wave goodbye to her new best friend one last time.

"Come back soon," yelled Sofia.

"I promise," said the alien.

Back in her bedroom, Sofia unzipped her rucksack and stared in surprise at the sparkling Moon rock the alien had left for her.

She gazed back up at the starry sky, hoping that her next BIG adventure would be out of this world.

GO DIVING?
Maybe I'll ...

Sofia, look out for more **Mini Adventures** books.
Go to www.orangutanbooks.com

Story by J.D. Green
Illustrated by Jo Lindley
Designed by Ryan Dunn

First published by Orangutan Books in 2019
1 Queen Street, Bath BA1 1HE

www.orangutanbooks.com
Follow us @orangutanbooks

ISBN 978-1-78979-691-9

Printed in Italy
OB_PO201990